LIVE ON PURPOSE

90 WAYS TO JUMP-START YOUR INSPIRED LIFE

TASHAI LOVINGTON

TARAZOD
PRESS

For more by Tashai Lovington, go to her website at:

https://tashai.net

Cover design: © 2024 by Tashai J. Lovington

Copyright 2024 by Tarazod Press LLC

ISBN: 979-8-9861947-4-5 (softcover)

Praise for Tashai Lovington

"I think a lot of people need to take advantage of this. I'm thrilled that you are doing the work, because it's so needed."
—**Jack Canfield,** New York Times Best Selling Author of *The Success Principles* and Co-creator of the #1 Best Selling book series *Chicken Soup for the Soul*

"Tashai is so encouraging and inspires you to live a better life!"
—**James Malinchak**, featured on ABC's Hit TV show, "Secret Millionaire", Founder, www.BigMoneySpeaker.com

"This book is the secret weapon and blueprint that every person or professional can use to achieve happiness and success in their business, their career and in their life. Tashai Lovington has put together a unique collection of life's lessons, and success strategies to help you be the best person you can be. Her book is incredibly noteworthy, valuable and inspiring to help you learn how to never give up on yourself, overcome challenges and shine your life to the fullest now!"
—**John Formica, The "Ex-Disney Guy",** America's customer experience speaker at JohnFormica.com

"This wonderful book shows you how to unlock your full potential and get the very most out of yourself." —**Brian Tracy,** President of Brian Tracy International and author *Maximum Achievement* and *Eat That Frog*

"These concepts are fundamental for those looking to get the life they've always dreamed of."

—**Kevin Harrington**, Original Shark from **Shark Tank**

"Tashai teaches you to believe in yourself and that the universe has your back." —**Patty Aubery**, 14 time *New York Times* Best Selling Author, Co-creator of **Chicken Soup For The Soul** Enterprises, President of The Canfield Training Group

"Take your life to the next level! Tashai offers invaluable techniques and exercises to finally achieve the success you've always wanted" —**Jill Lublin**, Master Publicity, Strategist, 4x best-selling author.

"Tashai Lovington has mastered the art of engagement by capturing the reader's attention from the first page all the way through to the end. She has taken her own life experiences and her astute observations and skillfully incorporated them into insightful spiritual life lessons."
—**Sue Corbin,** Author, Speaker, & Trainer

Motivate and Inspire Others!

"Share this Book"

Special quantity discounts

To place an order contact:
https://tashai.net

INTRODUCTION

Do not feel lonely, the entire
universe is inside you.
Stop acting so small. You are
the universe in ecstatic
motion. Set your life on fire.
—Rumi

In my earlier book, *Fill the Gap: How to Manifest From Where You Are Now to the Life You Want*, I shared stories and techniques on how to use universal principles to create the successful life you desire. Let's go further!

If you are serious about changing or improving your current situation, and I know you are, *Live on Purpose* will take you to the next level. Within these pages are 90 distinct entries containing short exercises, self-empowering affirmations, and cutting edge insights into aligning yourself with the life you want.

Designed specifically for the person who is ready now to take the next step, this book is meant to be read every day. Keep it next to your bedside or by your favorite reading spot. Let go of resistance, find your consistency, and be in the moment. Your life is about to change.

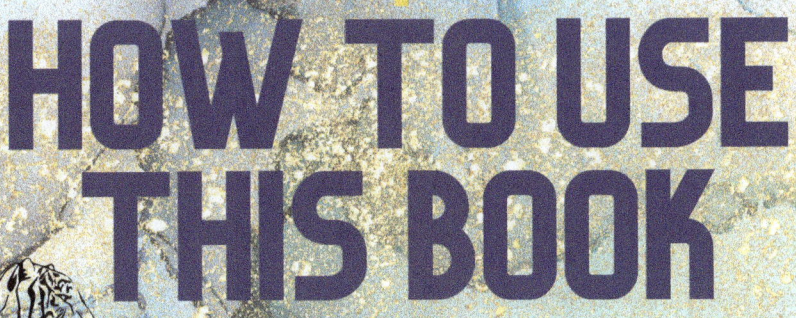

HOW TO USE THIS BOOK

Method 1 - Start at the beginning and read one entry per day for 90 days. I suggest making it part of your morning practices, to be ingested before heading off for your daily activities. One page per day. Take your time. Incorporate what you are reading. After three months, you will have assimilated the full scope of lessons and mindset-realignment. You will be a different person. Then if you choose, you can begin again back at the first entry for another round. But this time, your perspective will have changed. You'll see the content with new eyes. Expect that it will hit you at a deeper level ... because it will.

Method 2 - You can also use this book as a tool to connect with your higher guidance, like a personal oracle. Each morning, open up to a random page to receive specific direction for that day.

No matter how you choose to utilize this book, this is not about efforting. Yes, you will take action. However, it will be inspired action. Do the exercises, absorb the lessons, and allow the affirmations to work for you. This is going to feel like fun, not hard work.

Go get 'em tiger!

1

DREAM BIG

*If you have the ability to imagine it,
or even to think about it, this universe
has the ability and the resources to
deliver it fully unto you.*
—Abraham-Hicks

2

GET QUIET

Listen for the guidance from within—not the fearful ego—but the voice of your inner being. How do you know the difference? Easy. How do you feel? Excited? Inspired? Happy? Then trust it! These are the emotions of your true self.

SET THE TONE FOR THE DAY

Engage in an early morning meditation.

Exercise:

Take 10-15 minutes. Sit in a **comfortable** spot in your home, out in nature, or any place you feel at ease. **Gently** breathe in and out. And listen. Pick a sound and use it as a focal point. Doesn't matter what it is, could be a window fan, **bird song**, or traffic on the highway. If your thoughts wander, gently bring your focus back to the sound. With just a little **consistency**, you'll feel greater ease and the results will be profound. Your life will begin to shift.

4

YOU ARE NOT ALONE

You have a support team. It comes to your assistance in both a physical and non-physical manner, even if you are not yet aware of it. Start looking and feeling for signs of support in your life.

Affirmation:

I am directly **connected** to my higher self who knows exactly what I want and how best to **achieve** it. I allow my **guidance** to come to me.

5

BELIEVE IN YOURSELF

It's time.

Affirmation:

I am so much **more** than who I've been told I am. **Within** me is the power to change my world. I **believe**.

6
YOU HAVE INNER GUIDANCE

Are you feeling joyful? Uplifted? Then follow that intuition.

Intuition is a direct signal from your deepest self that you are navigating from your true center.
—Gay Hendricks

FILL THE GAP

What is the gap? It's the discrepancy between the vibration you are currently resonating with and the one you would have if you were living the life of your dreams.

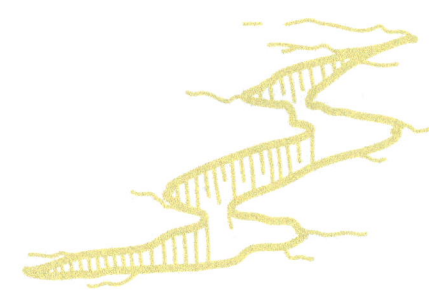

Exercise:

As we know from **quantum** physics, everything is energy. On a molecular level, everything is **vibrating**. The more in sync we are with our true nature of love and joy, the higher the **frequency**. Raise your vibration today by **daydreaming** about something that fills you with bliss.

8

YOU WILL KNOW

When you're ready, you will know. It's like turning on a light. You suddenly see all the possibilities in front of you, where before you weren't even aware they existed.

Affirmation:
I know what I want, and the **universe** is engaged right now with bringing it to me. I am open to the exciting **possibilities** all around me.

9
DON'T GIVE UP

The difference between those who have manifested their dreams and people who have not is often just a matter of perseverance.

Hold to your dreams of a better life and stay committed to striving to realize it.
-Earl G. Graves, Sr.

ENJOY YOURSELF

The choice to feel good is always yours to make, really. You are the master of your own thoughts.

Affirmation:

I deserve to feel joy in my life. I allow myself to be happy.

11

YOUR CHOICE

There are two ways to be remembered, as an inspiration or as a horrible warning. You decide.

Affirmation:

My life is a shining example.

I belong here.

12

BELIEFS ARE NOT LAWS

What you believe defines your experiences. Change your beliefs and your life will transform.

Exercise:

Make a list of your top five goals. Think big here. Write them down as if nothing is out of reach, anything is possible. When you're done, how do you feel? **Excited**? inspired? Or do you, instead, just feel worse? How you feel is an **indication** of your beliefs. The good news is you can change your beliefs to reflect the life you want. Start today by acting as if you've already reached your goals. Feel the **good feelings**. And just as importantly, begin looking for and acknowledging little **signs** of your dreams becoming **reality**. As your beliefs shift, so will your experience of life.

13

REPLENISH YOURSELF

Go to that quiet place, let chaos drop. Feel the steady rhythm of your breath, the movement of your blood through your heart. Let loose the reins and drift awhile. Listen for inspiration. If an idea comes while you're in this receptive state, act on it. Take a step in that direction and see what unfolds.

Let yourself be silently drawn by the strange pull of what you really love. It will not lead you astray. —Rumi

14

NURTURE YOUR DREAMS

Exercise:
Have a goal, and **be specific** about when you would like to achieve it. From now until that future date, **ask yourself** each evening, "What five things did I do today towards **reaching** my goal?" Write out your answers so you can track your **progress**.

BUILD MOMENTUM

Step by step. Be gentle with yourself. You will get there. It's time to start believing.

Affirmation:
I am moving in the direction of my dreams. Everyday new and exciting opportunities are available to me. I have the support of the entire universe at my beck and call.

16

YOUR MIND IS YOUR BUFFER OR YOUR BANE

You decide how you feel about the things around you, and this creates your life experience.

Exercise:

You can't just not think a negative thought. However, you can **choose** instead to switch focus. Look for **uplifting** things in your life you can **appreciate** right now. Place your attention there. Even if it's just the **simple** knowledge that the sun came up this morning and you have **breath** in your lungs. Focus is a choice and it's yours to make. Choose right now.

LET THIS DECADE BE YOUR TIME

17

Don't settle. Keep moving in the direction of your dreams.

Exercise:

Start your **bucket list**. This is your list of things you want to accomplish before you kick the bucket. **Write** down at least 100 ideas. Nothing is too big or too small. If you've **already** created a bucket list, review it, and don't be afraid to **update** it if your interests have evolved.

18

TURN FEAR ON ITS HEAD

What's that one thing you've wanted to do but were afraid of trying?

Do the thing you fear the most and the death of fear is certain. —Mark Twain

19

LOVE YOURSELF

Exercise:

Look in the mirror. Gaze into your eyes and repeat this **affirmation**. I love you. If that's too new or uncomfortable, start with, I am **learning** to love you. With practice, you will come to know just what it means to really **love yourself**. And when you do, your world will reflect this back to you in all aspects of your life.

20

NO JUDGEMENT

Your greater non-physical self is always with you. It is you. It knows everything you have ever done, your innermost thoughts and desires. There is no judgment. No criticism. It loves you without condition. Does that surprise you? It shouldn't. You are loved.

Affirmation:
I deserve love.
I am loved.

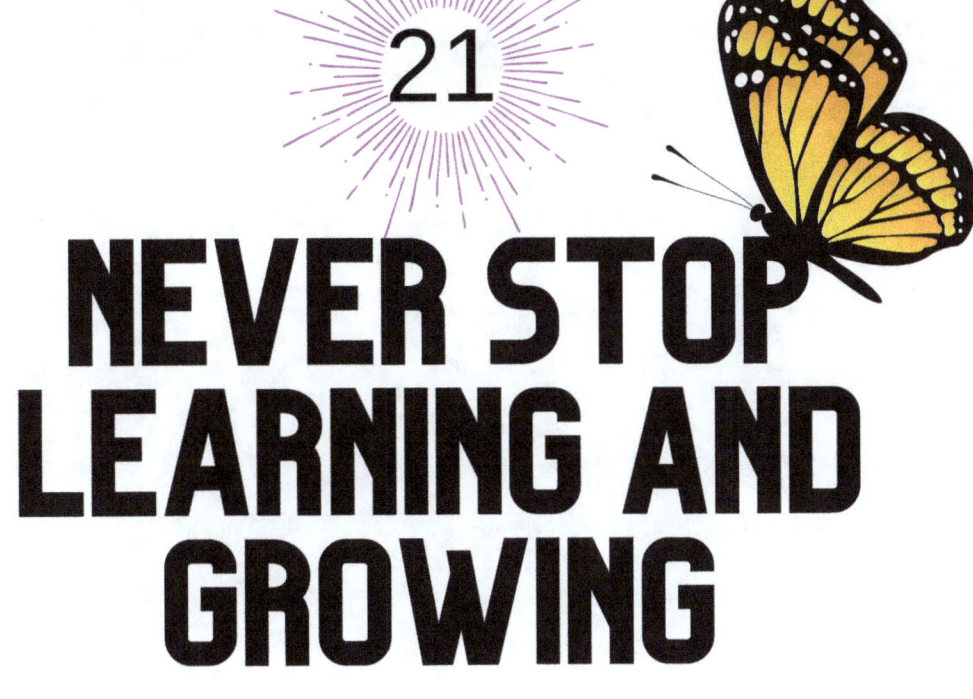

21

NEVER STOP LEARNING AND GROWING

When you are inspired and excited to be here in this world, you are attracting life force to you.

❖

Exercise:

Expand your mind and/or body in some way today. Read for 15 minutes in an educational or **inspirational** book. Listen to a podcast. Sign up for a webinar. Add a new **exercise** to your workout routine. Take a watercolor class. Visit an art or natural history museum. Identify the birds singing outside your window. **Choose** something that feels good to you.

22

FIND YOUR INSPIRATION

Imagination is everything,
it is the preview of life's
coming attractions.
—Albert Einstein

HONE YOUR FOCUS

Exercise:
Set a timer for two minutes. Then close your eyes and **visualize** something you want. **Seeing** it is a start, but feeling the feeling is more important. What does it feel like when you have it?

Do this on a **consistent** basis and you will train yourself to focus on the good feelings no matter what **life situation** you find yourself in.

YOU ARE IN
CONTROL

You are in control of your own thoughts, which in turn, directly affect your vibrational frequency. This is true whether it is done unconsciously or through deliberate choice.

Affirmation:
I control my thoughts, therefore I can change my life.

25
YOU ATTRACT

You attract the vibrational equivalent to whatever you focus on day after day.

See yourself living in abundance and you will attract it. It always works, it works every time, with every person.
—Bob Proctor

STOKE THE FIRE OF YOUR PASSIONS

Exercise:

Spend some time today writing down things you love doing or experiencing. Have fun with it. In these are the seeds of your destiny.

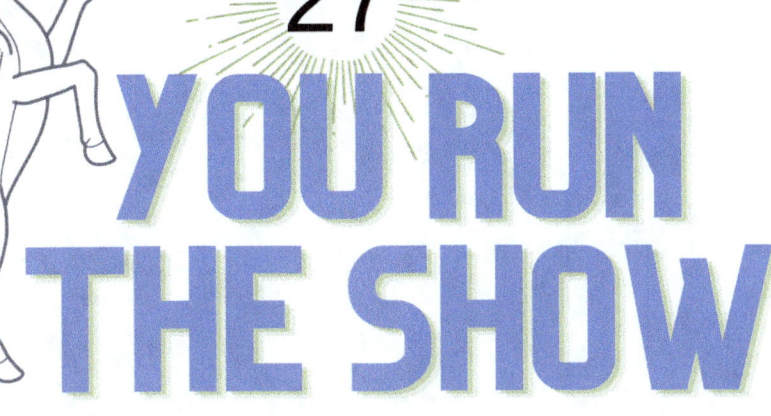

27
YOU RUN THE SHOW

Are you choosing your way or living by default?

Affirmation:
I am the maker of my life.
I expect greatness.

28

TAKE STEPS

When inspiration hits, follow it. That's when the door of opportunity is open at its widest.

Exercise:

Act when inspired to, even if it scares you. Take one step in that direction and see if the inspiration still feels true. If it does, keep moving.

29

EACH DAY BRINGS OPPORTUNITY

Sometimes just getting out of bed in the morning is a success. Acknowledge it.

Affirmation:

I live in the **present** moment and also look forward to what's coming next. I **celebrate** the little things, and I honor myself for being here.

30
YOU CREATE YOUR OWN FUTURE

When you shift your mindset to embrace the idea that you alone are 100% responsible for what comes into your life, buckle up. It's going to be a fun ride.

When I look at the future, it's so bright it burns my eyes.
—Oprah Winfrey

31

APPRECIATE EVERYTHING YOU HAVE

By practicing appreciation, you raise your vibration. In turn, you attract other people, things, and events into your life that sync with this vibratory frequency.

Exercise:

Fill in the following blanks.

I appreciate_____
because _____.

Repeat this five times today.

32

YOU ARE CLOSER THAN YOU KNOW

When the feeling of hopefulness bubbles up inside, it's a signal that your dreams are in the process of becoming a reality. Optimism and knowing are not far off. Do not let your current reality dissuade you from delighting in this vibratory state of positivity.

Affirmation:
I can have the life of my dreams. Anything is possible. I believe.

33
HAVE COMPASSION FOR YOURSELF AND OTHERS

Affirmation:

I am doing the best I can right now and so is everyone else. I am where I am, and no matter what, I am worthy.

34
SOMETIMES ALL IT TAKES IS A LITTLE KINDNESS

Be KIND

Carry out a random act of kindness, with no expectation of reward, safe in the knowledge that one day someone might do the same for you.
—Princess Diana

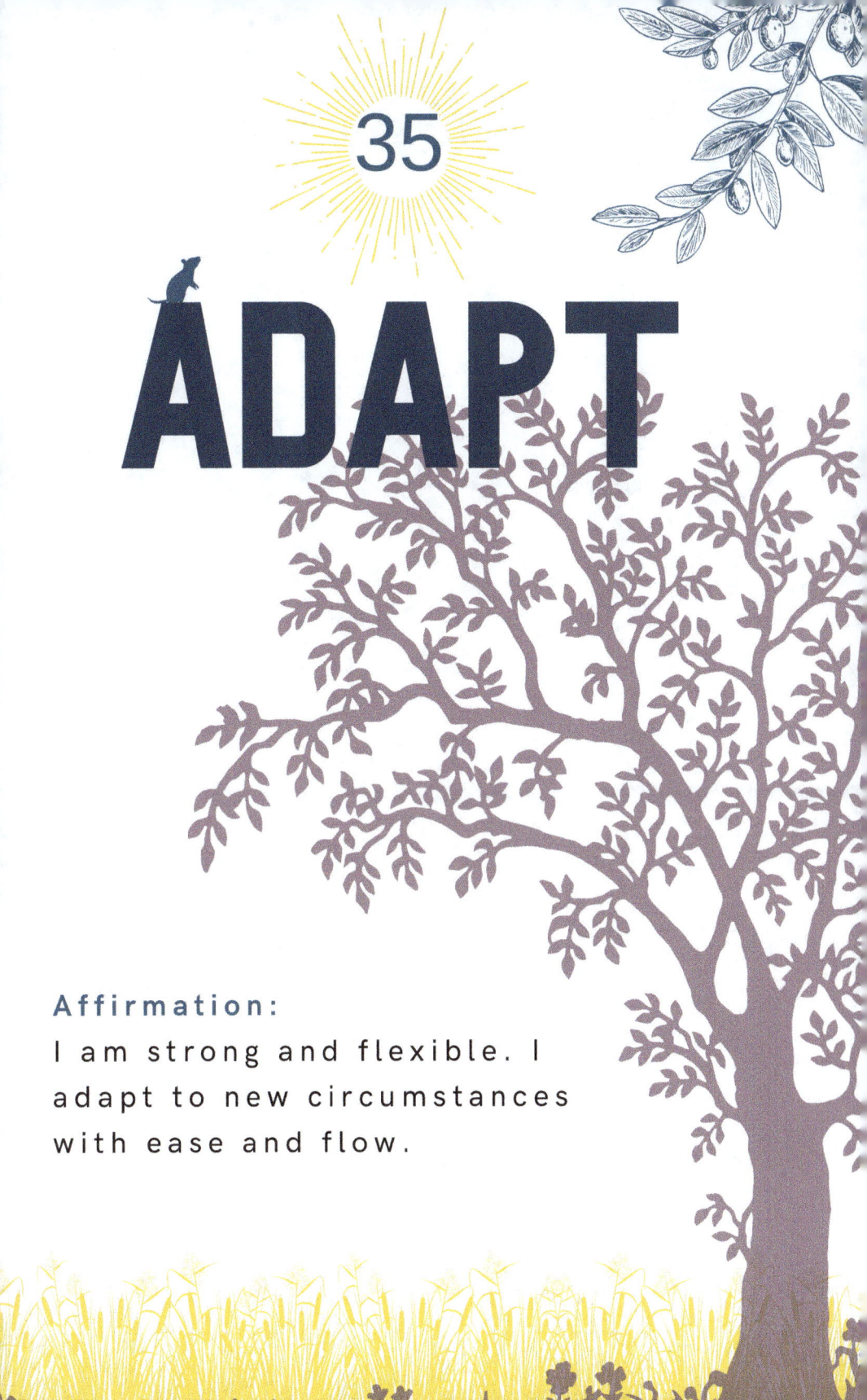

35

ADAPT

Affirmation:

I am strong and flexible. I adapt to new circumstances with ease and flow.

PRACTICE UPGRADING

Everyone has areas in life they would like to level up. The more you connect to the vibration of your true self, the greater the unfolding.

Exercise:
Do an upgrade. You are a **creative**, ever-evolving being. It's natural to look for ways to **improve** your circumstances, whatever they may be. Pick something in your life that you have been **putting up with**, something that bothers you, but you haven't taken the time to do anything about. Now's the time.

For example, if you dislike your bath towels—they might be cheap, tattered, or **simply** not your style anymore—get rid of them. Donate or **recycle** (depending on their condition). Now buy yourself a nice replacement set. This doesn't have to cost a lot. I'm not advocating wasteful spending. But there are times when the best thing you can do for **yourself** is to level up. Just pick something. Then in a month or so, pick something else.

FEEL THE LIFE FORCE IN NATURE

I feel you super moon,
Shining down on me.
There is extra energy in the air tonight
You call me to be aware.
Aware of how I feel,
Illuminating any darkness.
A friend in the night,
You hold the light.
Reflecting it back to me,
You see me in my beauty.
When I see it too,
I transcend that which doesn't serve me.

Lunar Affirmation:
I am connected to the natural rhythms and cycles
of life. I am calm and at ease in everything I do.

38
LET YOUR LIFE SHINE

You cannot help the world
by diminishing yourself.
Become the person you
were meant to be.

*The more light you allow within you, the brighter
the world you live in will be. —Shakti Gawain*

39

VISUALIZE GREAT THINGS

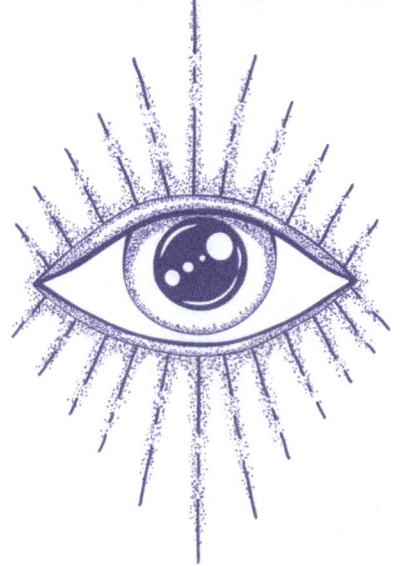

Exercise:

See your **best day** ever. What does it look like? Where are you? What are you doing? Who is there with you? **Feel** your way.

40

SLOW YOUR TRAIN

Abraham-Hicks shares an analogy of your life being like a speeding locomotive. If it's heading down the wrong track, you shouldn't try to instantly reverse direction. The momentum is too strong, and the results would be tremendously disruptive. Better to slow your train gently, and in very short order, you'll find yourself heading in the new direction of your dream life.

Truly, it doesn't take long; you will start noticing changes straight away. How do you accomplish this? By aligning with your true self. Notice the thoughts that feel good, follow them, and take action when inspired to do so. That's what you've been doing throughout this entire book.

Affirmation:
My life is ever-expanding with new **opportunities** for **fun**, excitement, and **surprise**.

41
COME BACK INTO ALLIGNMENT

The natural world is a phenomenal facilitator for finding the way back to your center.

Keep close to nature's heart...and break
clear away. once in a while. and climb a
mountain or spend a week in the woods.
Wash your spirit clean.
—John Muir

42

CHALLENGE WHAT YOU THINK YOU KNOW

Be open to the new and unexpected.

Affirmation:
I am open to learning new things and having fresh and wonderful experiences.

THE REAL YOU

Who you are is much greater than what you were led to believe.

Exercise:

Take a **moment** to sit and observe your body. How are you feeling right now? Are there any physical **sensations**? What are you sitting on and what does the surface feel like? Are you warm, cold, **comfortable**? Is there air flowing past your face? Take a few moments to relax into whatever you may be experiencing.

Now answer this: who is this **observer**? Beyond your body, there is an aspect of you that is **non-physical**. It, in fact, is the greater part of you, the eternal aspect of who you really are.

CONNECT WITH YOUR GUIDANCE

By allowing a little time each day for quiet introspection, you will reconnect with your higher guidance.

Affirmation:
Everyday I am learning, growing, and having fun. I am being guided to where I want to be.

45

FIND YOUR CENTER

See your accomplishment in making it this far, and feel the excitement for what's to come. Let life swirl around you, and know that for you, everything always works out.

Affirmation:
All is well in my world. Only good things come to me.

46

BREAKTHROUGH YOUR LIMITING BELIEFS

Be open to what's coming just around the corner. Author and speaker, Caroline Myss, mentions how with a shift in awareness, it's possible you might experience a sense of aloneness for a time as you acclimate to your new level of truth. Relationships change. Some may fade as you grow and evolve. Do not despair because …

always, new companions are found. No one is left alone for long.

47

BE WHO YOU REALLY ARE

Fulfillment **comes from expressing your** true self.

Affirmation:
It's safe to let my light shine and to be me.

48

Chill OUT

Exercise:

Spend 10 minutes today doing nothing. Don't do anything. Just be. Allow yourself this time without worry or guilt or distraction. Notice how you feel.

49

YOU ARE WHERE YOU NEED TO BE

Relax and enjoy the present moment. And know more fun and excitement are coming your way.

Affirmation:

My life is good. My **life** has **purpose**.
I'm in the right place at the right time.

50
KEEP MOVING FORWARD

Your life is changing, you are growing. Great things are in store no matter where you currently stand along your path.

Don't judge each day by the harvest you reap but by the seeds that you plant.
—Robert Louis Stevenson

51

MOVE YOUR BODY

Make a beeline to emotional improvement. Getting from despair to bliss is usually a multi-step process. Yet, the journey doesn't need to be long or difficult.

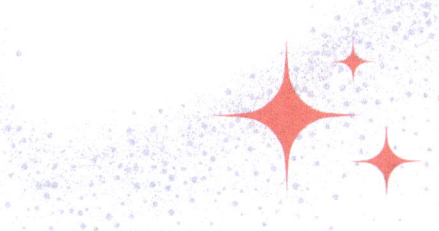

Exercise:
The next time you **find yourself** in an emotional funk, don't stay there. Move. I mean this **literally**, move your body. Try a minimum of 15-20 minutes of physical exercise. Walking, running, bicycling, swimming, skiing, yoga, pilates, rebounding, calisthenics, weight-lifting, boxing. The list goes on. Do whatever **feels right** for you and your fitness level. All that matters is to get your body moving. Endorphins will be **released**, your mood will improve, and you'll be on your way to feeling better.

52

TRUST

Affirmation:

Today, I trust that all I need is available to me. Everything always works out for me.

53
START WITH YOURSELF

When it comes to love, who needs it the most? Family? Friends? Neighbors? Raise your own hand. Because it's you! Of course you've heard it said that if you don't love yourself, you can't really love anyone else. News flash! It's true.

Love yourself first, and everything else falls in line. —Lucille Ball

54
LIGHTEN UP

We all can benefit from lightening up a little. Let go of something today that you've been holding on to for far too long. It could be a physical object you don't use or an old belief or behavior that no longer serves you.

Affirmation:
All that I need comes easily to me. I am light, happy, and free.

55

AFFIRM THE LIFE YOU WANT

Exercise:

Affirmations work best when your beliefs are aligned with your desires. Think about something you really want. Create a present-tense positive statement about it. Do it in such a way that your current paradigm expands but not so far that you end up focusing only on the lack of the thing you want. In other words, whatever you say, it must bring a good warm feeling of joy.

Example Affirmation:

I am enjoying the Pacific Ocean view from the veranda of my beautiful Spanish-style dream home.

56

ALLOW GOOD THINGS INTO YOUR LIFE

Allow yourself to be healthy.
Allow yourself to be loved and to love.
Allow your dreams to come true.

Affirmation:
I allow good things to come to me.

57

ACCEPT YOUR GREATNESS

Yep. If you are here on the planet, you have something to contribute. Own it baby.

Affirmation:
I am worthy of great things.
I have greatness within me.

58

FOCUS ON WHAT YOU WANT

Don't let yesterday take up too much of today. —Will Rogers

59
CELEBRATE
LOVE

You need no excuse to love, and I'm not only talking about the romantic variety. You can love your life, kids, family, friends, pets, and don't forget yourself. But hey, you can also love your car, eating a cheeseburger, or watching ducks.

Exercise:
Think about something you love and take a few minutes to really savor it. Enjoy the good warm feeling.

CONNECT THE DOTS

Being yourself—who you really are—is only truly possible when you align your physical self with the greater eternal you.

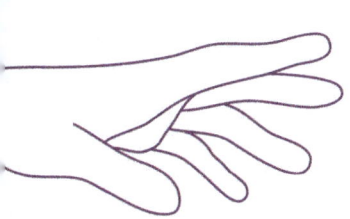

Affirmation:
There is more to me than meets the eye. I am an eternal being, and my life is filled with ease and joy.

61

DON'T TAKE LIFE SO SERIOUSLY

Enjoy your part and know everything will work out in the end.

As Shakespeare said, All the world's a stage and all the men and women merely players.

62

LET GO

Take a break from the overthinking,
overworking, and overdoing.
Sit. Breathe.
There are endless possibilities for your desires to
manifest. Stop looking for the *way* and start enjoying
the path you are on. And in doing so,
the way will find you.

Affirmation:
I love and accept myself just as I am.
Everyday and in every way, my life is
getting better and better.

63

GROWTH IS ON THE OTHER SIDE OF FEAR

Exercise:

Is there something you have been **wanting** to do but are too afraid to try? Do it within the safety of your own mind. **Visualize** yourself **accomplishing** it successfully and with ease. Really feel the good feeling of your success.

Now take an actual step towards that end today. Study, **practice**, send an email, make a call, sign up for a course. Take one action, see where that leads, and go forward from there. Fear **subsides** with knowledge and **understanding**.

64

HONOR YOURSELF

**ffirmation:**

My true self is kind, beautiful, and happy. I love who I am.

65
CELEBRATE THE LIGHT

Life is a contrast of light and shadow. Your great power lies in your freedom to choose where you place your focus. If you want to be happy, your path is clear. Find the good in all things. The more often you do this, the greater the attraction will be for more blissful people, things, and circumstances to show up on your doorstep.

Keep your face always towards the sun and the shadows will fall behind you.
—Walt Whitman

DON'T BE AFRAID TO ASK FOR HELP

No matter where you are in life, a good coach, teacher or mentor will help get you farther and faster to wherever it is you want to go.

Affirmation:

I attract the right **people** to **assist** me in attaining my **goals**.

REMEMBER TO *breathe*

Stressful emotions like anger and worry can act like a freeze ray, causing you to unknowingly hold your breath. The good news is that just the opposite is also true. If you consciously deep breathe during a stressful situation, your mental state will release and raise to a better feeling emotion. Breathe through the stress baby.

Exercise:
Take three **deep** breaths right now. For each, inhale, **breathe** in for four counts, "one-two-three-four." Pause for one count. Then breathe out for a count of six. Finally, **hold** for one more count. That's 4-1-6-1. Repeat two more times. Do you feel more **peaceful**? When your exhale is longer than the inhale, it sends a signal to your nervous system to relax.

FREEDOM IS YOUR NATURAL BIRTHRIGHT

Exercise:

When you are aligned with your true self, opportunity knocks, doors open, and life comes for you in unforeseen and exhilarating ways. You are free to be the person you truly are.

Affirmation:

I am the creator of my world. I control my own destiny. I am free to be me.

69

EMBRACE YOUR POWER

You are directly connected to the source of all there is. At your most grand, you are pure joy. Own it.

Affirmation:
I am always connected to my source. I am learning, evolving, and loving the adventure.

70

ATTITUDE IS EVERYTHING

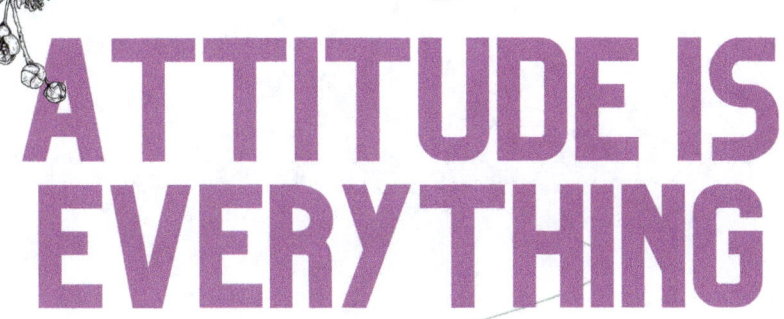

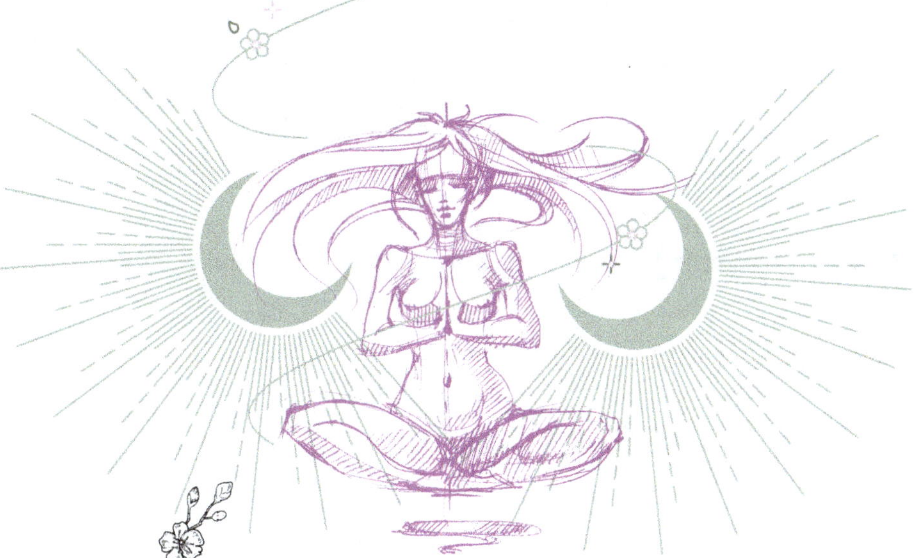

Change your attitude and you change your life.
—Roy T. Bennett

71

KNOW WHAT YOU WANT

With clarity comes focus and movement forward.

Exercise:
In previous exercises, I've asked you to write down your goals. Doesn't matter what they are, how unrealistic they may seem to the linear mind, or what others might think once you achieve them. Your desires are calling to you for a reason.

Now go further. It is important to review them regularly. As you grow, details may change, new ideas come, others fade. Don't be afraid to reevaluate what your dream life looks like. Today, spend a little time reassessing your goals, where you are now, and what you want things to look like in six months. Then stay alert to the opportunities when they arise.

72

AIM HIGH

Don't let doubt or fear
limit your dreams.
Think big.
Be bold.

Affirmation:
If I can dream it, I can do it.
I have the power to manifest
the life I want.

73

THE SECRET

Follow the thoughts that feel good, then act when inspired to. That, simply put, is the secret to life.

If you are working on something that you really care about, you don't have to be pushed. The vision pulls you.
— Steve Jobs

74

HAVE FUN

The world is a vast playground waiting for you to come explore. Within its sea of diversity, life never stops calling you forward. You can hear it beckoning, particularly when you are happy and feeling good. So consciously make a decision today to do something fun. Then be aware of any inspirations or ideas that come to your awareness.

Affirmation:
I live a **joyful** life. I am in sync with universal forces that **guide** me daily along my path.

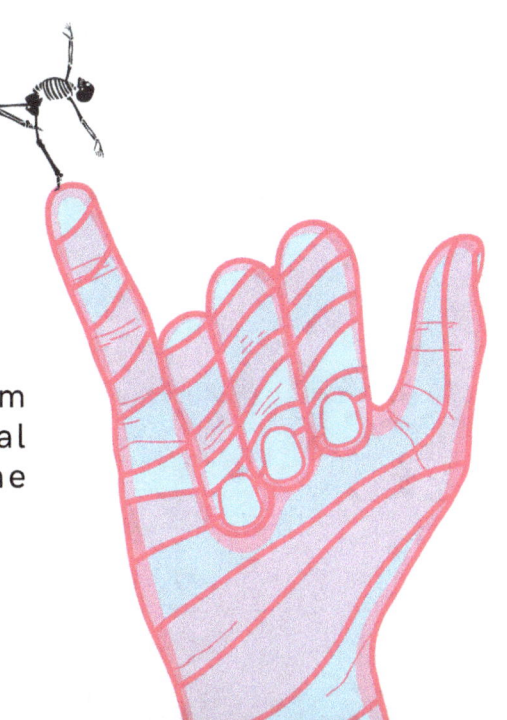

75

EMBRACE IT

Let go of resistance and embrace your personal power.

Affirmation:

I feel light, loose, flexible, and strong.
I am glad to be alive.

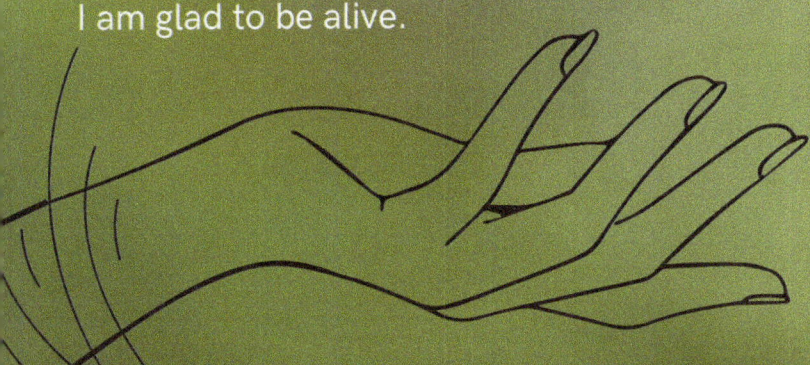

76
LET IT GO

Declutter your life. Experience how good it feels to free up space on a physical, psychological, and energetic level.

Exercise:

Start small. Pick one thing to go through and **declutter** today. A wallet, purse, kitchen junk drawer, office desk, the inside of your car. Sell, donate, **recycle** or discard anything you no longer use or need.

Keep only those things that you still find useful or that bring you **joy**. Once you've completed this task, take note of how much **lighter** you feel.

77

CHOOSE YOUR OWN ADVENTURE

When you take 100% responsibility for your own life, opportunities begin to materialize that were not visible to you before. Doors open. By relinquishing the act of placing blame on others (and self), new pathways forward are revealed, ones you didn't know were there. Begin today. Feel your way. It's your life and you are the master of it. Don't let anyone convince you otherwise.

Affirmation:
Life is a fun
adventure, and I am
ready for it.

78
FOCUS YOUR ATTENTION

Look for the successes that are in your life now, no matter how small.

The pessimist sees difficulty in every opportunity. The optimist sees opportunity in every difficulty.
—Winston Churchill

79
BE SELECTIVE

The thoughts that you think on a regular basis directly affect how you feel. And how you feel, in turn, influences what you actually perceive in your day-to-day life. When you learn to direct your focus more consistently in a manner that feels good, the outside world must change to match your new perception.

Exercise:

When you head out today, be conscious of your thoughts and actions. Observe how your mind travels as you encounter different stimuli. What you're feeling can change from one moment to the next.

If you happen to find yourself in some minor, yet undesirable situation, notice it, and gently introduce other thoughts, good-feeling ones that bring you back in line with who you really want to be. Before long, you'll come to a place where you can see the good in almost everything you encounter.

80

THE WORLD IS YOUR OYSTER

Change yourself
and the
world changes
with you.

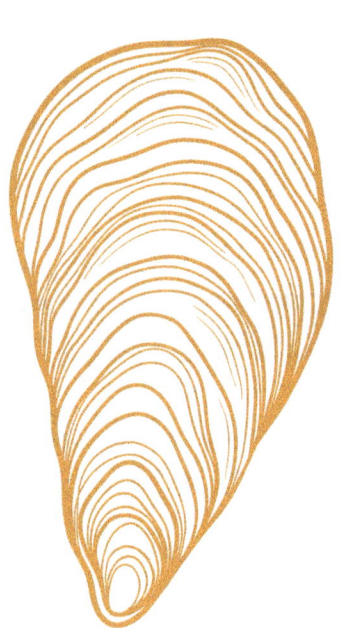

Affirmation:

I am aligned with my true nature. I can go
anywhere I want. I can do anything I want. I can
be anything I want.

ALL THINGS ARE POSSIBLE

Really. Take a moment to let that feeling sink in. You live in a universe where anything you can imagine can become reality.

For most people at this point, the linear mind is off to the races to find a thousand examples to the contrary, just to make clear that this couldn't possibly be true. But ask yourself why would you want to go there? Why is it so important to look for examples of the impossible? You'll never get to where you want to be with that mindset.

Transform your thinking. Start to believe in the possibilities and watch what happens in your life.

Impossible is not fact, it's an opinion. —Muhammad Ali

EMPOWER YOURSELF

Affirmation:

I am happy, healthy, wealthy, and free. I am aligned with my eternal self who calls me forward in every moment of my life.

83

YOU ARE FREE

This is true, no matter what your current life situation may be. Don't get entangled with what was or even what is. Place your attention firmly on what will be. Take action when inspired to. Then watch as universal forces bring it to you.

Affirmation:
My life is **joyous** and bountiful. I'm so **happy** I could _____ (fill in the blank)!

84
REALLY LIVE

You are here to live *your* life, not what someone else thinks is best for you. It's natural to want to please your loved ones, but be true to who you are too.

Exercise:

Take a few moments to really look at your **life**. Is the path you're on **fulfilling**? If not, avoid placing blame on others (or yourself). You don't need your family and friends to change in order for you to find your **bliss**. Simply focus your attention on what feels good to you right now, even if it appears to be diametrically opposed to what others want for you. The **universe** has a way of ironing out all the details to make it work for everyone involved. The key is to find the good feeling you are looking for and stay with it. You don't need to know how. Your non-physical self handles the details. Your job is to stay with the good feeling thoughts.

Practice this today. Think about something you really want to do. Feel it as if you're already living it. Consistently focusing in this fashion will open pathways to your goal in ways you can't yet **imagine**.

85

YOU CREATE YOUR LIFE

You create your world.

Two people step outside, encounter the same exact set of circumstances, and yet, come away with two totally different life experiences. One feels exhilarated by the wind on her face, the opportunities before her, and the people she meets. The other simply feels uncomfortable, bored, and annoyed. Neither is right or wrong. This is not about judgment.

A happy life is created. Start making your choices today. Small steps lead to great strides. And it happens fast. Be kind and gentle with yourself, especially if you stumble, but get back up and keep building your momentum.

Affirmation:
I can see my future and it is delightful.

86

LET GO OF THE PAST

What's done is done. Turn your focus to the now.
Take a step into your new life today.

*It's never too late to be
who you might have been.
—Mary Ann Evans
(pen name George Eliot)*

87

RELAX

Exercise:

Take a little time **today** to do nothing in particular. Sit outside and watch clouds pass. Put on some **soothing** music. Soak in a bath. Take a slow stroll through a nearby park or wood. **Lay** on your floor and listen to the gentle hum of the refrigerator or air conditioner. **Don't overthink** it. The point is to let go. Do something that feels good to you. The only **criteria** is that it be relaxing.

88

APPRECIATION IS A SUPERPOWER

When you recognize the value, beauty, and good that's all around you, it acts like a tractor beam and draws more of those things into your life.

Affirmation:

Life is good and I see the beauty that is all around me.

89

YES YOU CAN

You can have the life you want. It does not matter where you came from, how young or how old you are, how rich or poor, or the level of your education. Manifesting your desires has much more to do with aligning with your greater self, acting when inspired to, and allowing your manifestations in.

Affirmation:
I can have the life I want.
I am worthy. I belong
here.

90

LIVE ON PURPOSE

Breathe, relax, and feel joy in your heart. When you encounter unwanted experiences, gently bring your focus back to happier thoughts. Look for the good in your world. In doing so, you align with your true self. That's when the magic happens!

Never worry about what's coming for you. Just go get what you want by following the thoughts that feel good.
—Abraham-Hicks

CONCLUSION

If the methodologies in this book are working for you, I recommend starting over again at the beginning with entry number one. It's been 90 days. You are not the same person you were when you began. Your mindset has expanded and your possibilities multiplied. By re-reading the entries, you will notice new details and pick up fresh ideas. Keep going. There's more great things in store for you.

Peace out XOXO
– Tashai

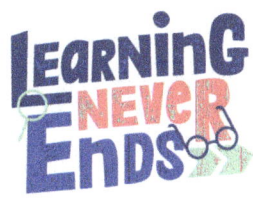

Acknowledgments

Over the years, many have shared ideas, support or mentoring that has impacted my life, each in their own way. It's impossible to thank everyone and I apologize for anyone I have inadvertently not listed. Please know that I do greatly appreciate you.

Special appreciation must go to: Joseph Campbell, Dr. Wayne Dyer, Louise Hay, Caroline Myss, Jack Canfield, Patty Aubery, Mike Dooley, Richard Bach, Esther and Jerry Hicks, Abraham Hicks, Darryl Anka and Bashar, James Redfield, Paramahansa Yogananda, Dr John Ryan, Ram Dass, The 14th Dalai Lama, Edgar Cayce, Kevin Todeschi, Denise Linn, Julia Cameron, James Malinchak, Hal Elrod, Nick Ortner, and Brad Yates.

About the Author

Tashai Lovington is a #1 bestselling author, course-creator, coach, speaker, and spiritual intuitive. She has appeared on public television and her work has been written up in numerous newspapers and periodicals. She was drawn to the study of new consciousness at a very early age which set her on a life-long adventure of discovery. Her work follows in the footsteps of some of the greatest teachers of leading-edge thought. She understands and implements the universal principle of attraction with deliberate intent in all areas of her life. Above all else, she has come to know that our natural state of being is one of joy and that the essence of life is to have fun.

For more of her books, courses, and body of work, visit her website: https://tashai.net

 youtube.com/@tashai.travels

 facebook.com/tashai.travels1

instagram.com/tashai.travels

Additional Books by Tashai

Fill The Gap: How to Manifest From Where You Are Now to the Life
You Want

Life-Mastering Habit Tracker [full-color version]

Life-Mastering Habit Tracker [black and white version]

Special FREE Resources For You

To help you achieve more success, there are FREE RESOURCES for you at:

https://www.freegiftfromtashai.com